33 THE SERIES™

AUTHENTIC MANHOOD

VOLUME **6** TRAINING GUIDE

A **MAN** AND HIS FATHERHOOD

A **MAN** AND HIS **FATHERHOOD**

Published by Authentic Manhood • © 2015 Fellowship Associates Inc. • Reprinted November 2021

ISBN 978-1-4300-3950-1 • Item 005717350

Project Management & Art Direction: Rachel Lindholm
Design: Samantha Corcoran, Mike Robinson, Details Communications, Lindsey Woodward
Editors: JoNell Calwell, Rick Caldwell, Grant Edwards, Rachel Lindholm, Sadie Smith, Steve Snider, Rebekah Wallace
Contributors: Rick Caldwell, Brian Goins, Tierce Green, Stephen James, Tim Kimmel, Meg Meeker, Beth Snider, Chase Snider, Jack Snider, Shelby Snider, Steve Snider, David Thomas, Paul Tripp

Authentic Manhood, Men's Fraternity and 33 The Series are registered trademarks of Fellowship Associates Inc.

To order additional copies of this resource, go to AuthenticManhood.com or Lifeway.com.

Printed in the United States of America

Distributed by:

Authentic Manhood
12115 Hinson Road, Suite 200
Little Rock, AR 72212

Groups Ministry Publishing
Lifeway Resources
One Lifeway Plaza
Nashville, TN 37234

How to Experience 33 as an Individual or Group

33 The Series can be viewed on DVD, downloaded from **authenticmanhood.com**, or experienced via mobile apps. Any of these three delivery systems can be utilized by groups or individuals. *One of the great things about this series is the variety of ways it can be used and/or presented.*

The series is organized in a way that provides flexibility and offers a variety of options on how the material can be experienced. *33* is organized into six topically-themed volumes that include six sessions each. *Volumes include topics on a man's design, story, traps, parenting, marriage, and career.* You can choose to commit to one volume/topic at a time, by limiting a particular experience to six sessions, or you can combine multiple volumes into one expanded experience that includes more sessions (12, 18, 24, 30, or 36). You can also choose any combination thereof.

However you choose to experience 33, the manhood principles and practical insights taught in each volume are essential for every man on the journey to Authentic Manhood. 33

How to Make the Most of Your 33 Experience

33 The Series is more than just a video series for you to watch and then mark off your list. When experienced with other men, it can be the pathway to Authentic Manhood that changes your life forever. Authentic Manhood is truly a movement that you can become a part of and then passionately invite others to join.

1 **Make sure you have a team.** Your experience will be greatly enhanced if you form a team with other men or at least one other man to help process the truths that you receive.

2 **Make sure every man has a 33 Training Guide.** A 33 Training Guide will enable men to take notes, record a strategic move after each session, and create an action plan at the end. It also contains articles, interviews, and features that will support the truths men receive from the video teaching.

3 **Make sure you stay caught up.** All the sessions of 33 can be purchased online and downloaded for only a few dollars per session. If you are viewing 33 with a group and miss a session, you can download the session you missed and stay caught up. (Purchase downloads at *www.authenticmanhood.com*)

Most importantly...

4 **Make sure you pass on the truths you learn to other men.** When session six ends, the exciting part just begins. Don't just sit back and wait for another study. Instead step up and find another man or group of men to lead through the volume you just completed. For a small investment of just a few dollars, you can download your very own set of this series and use it to make a HUGE investment in the lives of other men.

PLAY

33 is a resource that can set you up to influence the lives of other men tremendously.

Going through **33** yourself should be only the beginning.

After you complete this volume, download the videos at
AUTHENTICMANHOOD.com
for just a few dollars
and take another man or group of men through the series.

BIG

REJECT PASSIVITY
ACCEPT RESPONSIBILITY
LEAD COURAGEOUSLY
INVEST ETERNALLY

LIVE IT OUT!

Authentic Manhood

EXPERT PRESENTERS

Session 2- Grace Based

Session 3- True Greatness

Dr. Tim Kimmel
FAMILYMATTERS.NET

Dr. Tim Kimmel is the founder and Executive Director of Family Matters, whose goal is to see families transformed by God's grace into instruments of reformation and restoration. He believes the best way to pass on saving faith and a transformed life is within the nurturing confines of a loving home. To help others achieve this, he has developed resources, conferences, and media tools to equip and encourage parents, grandparents, churches, and couples. Tim and Family Matters conduct the Grace Based Parenting Conference across the country on the unique pressures that confront members of today's families. Tim has authored many books including:

RAISING KIDS FOR TRUE GREATNESS

GRACE BASED PARENTING

Welcomes Our
FATHERHOOD

Session 4- Sons

Stephen James and David Thomas

Stephen James and David Thomas are therapists, speakers, and the authors of *Wild Things: The Art of Nurturing Boys*. They are frequent contributors on ABC Family's *Living the Life* and *Moody's Midday Connection*. Their writings have appeared in numerous publications, including *Discipleship Journal*, *Relevant* and *Pastors.com*

Session 5- Daughters

Dr. Meg Meeker
MEGMEEKERMD.COM

Dr. Meg writes with the know-how of a pediatrician and the big heart of a mother because she has spent the last 30 years practicing pediatric and adolescent medicine. Her work with countless families over the years served as the inspiration behind her best-selling book: *Strong Fathers, Strong Daughters*. Dr. Meg has recently released *The Strong Parent Project* which uncovers the 12 Principles to raising great kids.

The Presenters

BRYAN CARTER

Bryan Carter taught the original Men's Fraternity curriculum to a group of more than 800 men over a three-year period at Concord Church. Additionally, he has been a frequent speaker at local and international churches, conferences, and events.

Bryan is the Senior Pastor of Concord Church in Dallas, Texas.

He is the author of a 28-day devotional book entitled *Great Expectations*. Bryan also contributed to the book *What Two White Men of God Learned from Black Men of God*, co-authored by Dr. Joel Gregory and Dr. Bill Crouch.

A recreational basketball player, Bryan is a fan of the NBA's Dallas Mavericks.

Bryan and his wife Stephanie are the parents of two daughters, Kaitlyn and Kennedy, and one son, Carson.

TIERCE GREEN

Tierce Green is Pastor of House Churches at Church Project in The Woodlands, Texas where his primary role is to call men up and equip them to lead and care for people. He also travels extensively as a speaker at conferences and training events. He taught the principles of Authentic Manhood to over a thousand men each week over a seven-year period in a seasonal gathering called The Quest.

Tierce created and produced a 12-session video series for men called *Fight Club: Some Things Are Worth Fighting For*. He has also written curriculum for Student Life and LifeWay.

A lifelong Dallas Cowboys fan, Tierce's favorite activities include landscaping, grilling just about anything, and having good conversations.

He and his wife Dana were married in 1987. They have one daughter, Anna.

JOHN BRYSON

Seeing firsthand the impact the original Men's Fraternity curriculum had on his own life, John Bryson decided to teach the material himself. In the years since, he has led thousands of men through the basic ideas of biblical manhood.

John is a co-founding teaching pastor of Fellowship Memphis in Memphis, Tennessee.

In 2010, he completed his Doctor of Ministry from Gordon-Conwell Theological Seminary. John is also the author of *College Ready,* a curriculum for college students, and travels the country consulting and investing in churches, church planters, leaders, and new ideas.

A native of Harlan, Kentucky, John played baseball at Asbury College.

He and his wife Beth have 6 children: Brooke, Beck, Bo, Boss, Blair, and Bayne.

Foundation

SESSION ONE | Training Guide

Foundation <small>Presented by Tierce Green</small>

I. INTRODUCTION

1. Fatherhood can make a man's life rich, filled with joy and laughter and give a man a lasting sense of gratification and achievement.

2. However, the reality is that being a father and cultivating a family isn't _____easy_____.

3. We need men who are willing to embrace the long road of building and _____cultivating_____ a family.

II. FIVE FOUNDATIONAL TRUTHS OF FATHERHOOD

1. The family was _____God's_____ idea.

   • The family was God's idea and was part of his purpose for mankind and for how we should relate to one another in this world.

      "Therefore a man shall leave his father and his mother and hold fast to his wife, and they shall become one flesh"
      Genesis 2:24 (ESV)

   God calls children a _____gift_____.

      "Behold, children are a heritage from the LORD, the fruit of the womb a reward. Like arrows in the hand of a warrior are the children of one's youth. Blessed is the man who fills his quiver with them! He shall not be put to shame when he speaks with his enemies in the gate."
      Psalm 127:3-5 (ESV)

- ___*Fatherhood*___ is not just some added to-do on your list of responsibilities.

2. Fatherhood is a God-given ___~~comission~~ ~~commision~~___ commission.

   - God has commissioned and entrusted fathers with the noble task of nurturing, guiding, and equipping their children for life.

   - This commission is taught directly or implied throughout the Bible. For example: Proverbs 22:6; 29:17; Deuteronomy 6:4–9; Ephesians 6:1–4; 1 Timothy 3:4.

   - "Parents ought to consider themselves entrusted with the (temporary) responsibility and stewardship of nurturing and cultivating a child's heart and mind in light of the Scriptures and on behalf of God. . . . [and] while children ought to obey both parents, fathers bear special responsibility for disciplining their children."
     - Andreas K. Kostenberger, *God, Marriage, and Family* [1]

3. Fatherhood takes ___*intentionality*___.

   - Authentic Manhood definition, which we discovered from the life of Jesus :

     o   Reject Passivity

     o   Accept Responsibility

     o   Lead Courageously

     o   Invest Eternally

[1]Andreas J. Köstenberger, *God, Marriage, and Family* 2d ed. (Wheaton: Crossway, 2010), 118, 125.

SESSION ONE | FOUNDATION

4. Wise fathers focus on the ___heart___.

"Never fully knowing ourselves, never fully knowing others, and never fully finding the abundant life . . . We spend our existence toiling to make life happen, and all it gets us is a grave, a marker, and a date."

– Chip Dodd , *The Voice of the Heart* [1]

• Heart-deficient fathers can be ___toxic___ for kids.

• Wise fathers focus on the hearts of their kids.

  o Parents are typically tempted to focus only on ___external___ behavior.

  o The Bible emphasizes the heart as the key to change and to full, abundant living.

    "Keep your heart with all vigilance, for from it flow pthe springs of life."
    Proverbs 4:23 (ESV)

    "The good person out of the good treasure of his heart produces good, and the evil person out of his evil treasure produces evil, for out of the abundance of the heart the mouth speaks."
    Luke 6:45 (ESV)

    "Behavior is not the basic issue. The basic issue is always what is going on in the heart. . . . The heart is the wellspring of life. Therefore, parenting is concerned with shepherding the heart." [2] – Tedd Tripp, Pastor

  o A thread that is going to run through this entire volume is the importance of connecting with your kids ___heart___.

[1]Chip Dodd, *The Voice of the Heart* (David T Dodd II, 2001) 5
[2]Tedd Tripp, *Shepherding A Child's Heart* (Shepherd Press, 1995), 4, 6.

5. Wise fathers are grace-dependent.

    • Wise fathers have recognized their own ___brokenness___ and their own need for forgiveness before a holy God.

        "All have sinned and fall short of the glory of God and are justified by his grace as a gift, through the redemption that is in Christ Jesus."

                                        Romans 3:23–24 (ESV)

    • Jesus tells us there is a link between expressing ___forgiveness___ and showing love.

        "... He who is forgiven little, loves little."

                                        Luke 7:47 (ESV)

    • Wise fathers also recognize their daily need for ___grace___ as a parent. They've realized they can't do it alone.

DISCUSSION / REFLECTION QUESTIONS

1. What would it look like in your fatherhood to apply our definition of Authentic Manhood?

   *Give more grace to the children.
   Love them regardless of their actions.
   Focus on your heart and their hearts*

2. Discuss the temptation to focus only on your kids' external behavior as opposed to focusing on the heart.

3. Discuss the importance of recognizing your own daily need for grace as a dad in light of offering that same grace to your kids.

*Grace is God's favor when we
really deserve his wrath.*

RESOURCES ON THE FOLLOWING PAGES:

- Loving a Prodigal (p. 18-21)

- Foundational Truths of Fatherhood (p. 22-23)

- Connecting to the Heart Resources (p. 24-25)

- THE RED ZONE: Fatherhood Statistics (p. 26-27)

LOVING A
PRODIGAL

BY BRIAN GOINS

What are you on today, Nic?

David asks his son as he drives his son's old Volvo. Nic huddles up against the passenger door, as far away from dad as he can physically be. The car is strewn with remnants of Nic's last bender: dirty jeans, a half-empty bottle of Gatorade, his leather jacket, empty beer bottles, a stale sandwich, and an intricately carved bong made of a glass beaker and meerschaum stem.

Nic attempts an apology, "I know I _____ up. I learned my lesson."

Nic's dad doesn't answer. Too many hollow words. Too many vain justifications.

"What are you on today, Nic?"

AN ANGRY WHISPER COMES FROM HIM,

"_____you."

David asked all the familiar questions:

DID I SPOIL HIM?

WAS I TOO LENIENT?

DID I GIVE HIM TOO LITTLE ATTENTION? TOO MUCH?

IF ONLY I HAD NEVER USED ALCOHOL OR DRUGS.

IF ONLY HIS MOTHER AND I HAD STAYED TOGETHER.

IF ONLY AND IF ONLY AND IF ONLY...

David highlights the social ignominy that bubbles to the surface when your child turns his or her back on your values, your love, and your family.

Parents toss and turn when their kids stray. We pour over Jesus' words in Luke 15 looking for some hidden script on loving our wayward children in such a way that our story ends in a raucous barbecue. But Jesus never offered a three step plan when he taught in parables. Jesus told stories about stuff from down here (lost coin, lost sheep, lost son) to describe stuff up there (kingdom of heaven, judgment, character of God). Here, Jesus used a universal story to talk about his Father to two very different groups of people (Luke 15:1-2). One group had turned the ten commandments into suggestions. The others mistook good behavior for a godly heart. So Jesus is targeting practical atheists and religious hypocrites more than anxious parents. However, if you find yourself sitting by the window praying for a reunion, Jesus reminds us there is never a pigsty too far from God's grace and relationship is far more important than righteousness.

FROM THE PIGS TO THE FATTED CALF

Sometimes the only thing a parent can do for a prodigal child is pray God brings them to a point where their stubborn heart seeks God. Even Solomon admitted that sin is fun...for a season. Until that season passes, whether that be months, years, or decades, Jesus reassures us that God values relationship more than righteousness.

THE OTHER PRODIGAL

Novelist Flannery O'Connor described a character who had, "A deep darkness in his heart because he saw that the best way to avoid Jesus is to avoid sin." In Luke 15, Jesus shows how it sometimes is easier to find God in the pigsty than the pew. The story speaks of two prodigals: one who abandoned his father out of selfishness and one out of self-righteousness. Both rebelled. One returned. As parents, we fear our kids running headlong into the more "public" pigsties than the private ones. Maybe because we can clearly see the baggage from a child who has a history

Dad, How do you love the familiar stranger?

of promiscuity more than a history of pride. But in this story Jesus highlights the possibility of living sanitized from sin, but not sanctified. Many have lived a righteous life without the righteousness of Christ. They've duped themselves into believing good behavior reflects a godly heart. For those kids, they will come to the end of days and hear the words, "Depart from me for I never knew thee."

What's worse, a season of sin or a lifetime of legalism? Perhaps your prodigal child left you because it was the only path to God.

Jesus reminded the religious Pharisees and scribes in the crowd (Luke 15:2), relationship is far more important to God than right living. When our kids stiff-arm our values, our beliefs, or our affection, Jesus illustrated a dad who never lost affection for his son despite his hateful actions. After his son slammed the door, the father kept the gate open, light on, and a feast on the back burner.

A friend of mine caught his son with some pot. Years before his son had walked away from his childlike faith. Now, in addition to debunking God, he was dabbling in drugs. For the past few years, the dad had sat in first row seats as his son

stumbled from one pigsty to the next.

But every Tuesday, they have lunch. As long as his son shows up, dad pays the tab. Dad doesn't enable. He puts up clear boundaries and holds his son's feet to the fire when he crosses them. He tries hard to not let his son's errant behavior or beliefs infringe on their relationship. Dad now cherishes those rare moments when his son lingers in the kitchen at night rather than secluding himself in his room.

Regardless of how well you parent, kids will choose their own path. If we judge God the Father by the performance of his kids, he'd never win parent of the year. For some, the only way to God's grace is through the doorway of depravity.

As a Dad, Loving the "familiar stranger" is messy.

There are no magic formulas, no rules, and no perfect plan because only God can break or soften a stubborn heart (1 Cor. 2:14-16). Such love requires fruit that doesn't naturally grow on our tree: love, joy, peace, patience, kindness, goodness, faithfulness, gentleness, and self-control. As parents of prodigals we live the gospel towards our kids and need the gospel to love our kids.

Foundational Truths of FATHERHOOD

01

02

03

04

05

FAMILY WAS GOD'S IDEA

"Behold, children are a heritage from the Lord, the fruit of the womb, a reward. Like arrows in the hand of a warrior are the children of one's youth. Blessed is the man who fills his quiver with them!" Psalm 127:3–5 (ESV)

FATHERHOOD IS A GOD-GIVEN COMMISSION

- Fathers are commanded to train up and discipline their children (cf. Proverbs 22:6; 29:17)
- Moses told parents to diligently teach the commands of the Lord to their sons and daughters (cf. Deuteronomy 6:4–9)

FATHERHOOD TAKES INTENTIONALITY

Authentic Men:
- Reject the cultural norm of the detached dad
- Accept the responsibility of this sacred commission
- Lead their families courageously regardless of setbacks or confusion

WISE FATHERS FOCUS ON THE HEART

- The heart is the wellspring of life (cf. Proverbs 4:23)
- "The good person out of the good treasure of his heart produces good, and the evil person out of his evil treasure produces evil, for out of the abundance of the heart the mouth speaks." Luke 6:45 (ESV)

WISE FATHERS ARE GRACE-DEPENDENT

Authentic Men recognize their own brokenness and need for forgiveness
- "All have sinned and fall short of the glory of God and are justified by his grace as a gift through the redemption that is in Christ Jesus." Romans 3:23 (ESV)
- Jesus says "He who is forgiven little, loves little." Luke 7:47 (ESV)

CONNECTING TO THE **HEART** RESOURCES

EMOTIONALLY HEALTHY SPIRITUALITY
PETER SCAZZERO

In this book, Scazzero outlines his journey and the signs of emotionally unhealthy spirituality. Then he provides seven biblical, reality-tested ways to break through to the revolutionary life Christ meant for you.

THE VOICE OF THE HEART
CHIP DODD

The Voice of the Heart offers a deeper understanding of how to live an abundant life. Chip Dodd teaches us how to begin to know our hearts so that we better know ourselves and are better equipped to live in relationship with others and, ultimately, with God.

SCARY CLOSE
DONALD MILLER

Scary Close is about the risk involved in choosing to impress fewer people and connect with more, about the freedom that comes when we stop acting and start loving. It is a story about knocking down old walls to create a healthy mind, a strong family, and a satisfying career.

THE GIFT OF BEING YOURSELF
DAVID BENNER

The self is not God, but it is the place where you meet God. Genuine self-knowledge revitalizes your spiritual life and opens the door to becoming who God has created you to be. Rest assured, you need not try to be someone you are not.

YOURUNIQUEDESIGN.COM

Just imagine how effective you would be if you could discover your unique, God-given design! Wouldn't it be awesome if every person could learn to maximize their special skills and abilities in service to him and to others? You will discover: How you have been wired by God, how you go about doing things, the lens through which you view life and what makes you come alive! A great tool for dads to better understand their kids' personalities (recomended for ages 13 and up).

FATHERHOOD STATISTICS

RESEARCH SHOWS WHEN A CHILD GROWS UP IN A FATHER-ABSENT HOME, HE OR SHE IS...

TWO TIMES
MORE LIKELY TO
DROP OUT
OF HIGH SCHOOL

MORE LIKELY
TO GO TO
PRISON

I IN 5 PRISON INMATES HA
A FATHER IN PRISON

4X
GREATER RISK
OF POVERTY

MORE LIKELY TO ABUSE DRUGS AND ALCOHOL

MORE LIKELY

TO HAVE
BEHAVIORAL PROBLEMS

SEVEN TIMES
MORE LIKELY TO GET
PREGNANT AS A TEEN

2X
MORE LIKELY
TO SUFFER FROM OBESITY

MORE LIKELY TO FACE ABUSE AND NEGLECT

http://www.fatherhood.org/bid/190202/The-Father-Absence-Crisis-in-America-Infographic

SESSION ONE | FOUNDATION

SCRIPTURE REFERENCES

Genesis 2:24 (NIV) "That is why a man leaves his father and mother and is united to his wife, and they become one flesh."

1 Timothy 3:4 (ESV) "He must manage his own household well, with all dignity keeping his children submissive."

Proverbs 4:23 (ESV) "Keep your heart with all vigilance, for from it flow the springs of life".

Luke 6:45 (ESV) "The good person out of the good treasure of his heart produces good, and the evil person out of his evil treasure produces evil, for out of the abundance of the heart his mouth speaks."

Romans 3:23-24 (ESV) "For all have sinned and fall short of the glory of God, and are justified by his grace as a gift, through the redemption that is in Christ Jesus."

Luke 7:47 (ESV) "Therefore I tell you, her sins, which are many, are forgiven—for she loved much. But he who is forgiven little, loves little."

SUPPORTING RESOURCES

Dodd, Chip. *The Voice of the Heart* (David T Dodd II, 2001) Page 5.

Köstenberger, Andreas J. *"God, Marriage, and Family"* 2d ed. (Wheaton: Crossway, 2010), Pages 118, 125.

Tripp, Tedd. *Shepherding A Child's Heart.* (Shepherd Press, 1995) Pages 4, 6.

* The content in the resources above does not necessarily reflect the opinion of Authentic Manhood. Readers should utilize these resources but form their own opinions.

Grace Based

SESSION TWO | Training Guide

Training Guide OUTLINE

Grace Based   Presented by Tim Kimmel

I. DAD'S JOB

1. The job of a dad is to connect to the ___*heart*___ of your child in such a way that it makes it easier for them to connect to the heart of God.

    *   Our heart connection to our kids is highly influenced by our heart connection with Jesus.

II. TYPES OF FATHERS

1. Fear-Based Fatherhood

    *   ___*Fear*___ cannot be our starting point in our role as a dad.

        "Courage is when you're scared to death but you saddle up anyway."
        -John Wayne[1]

2. Performance-Based Fatherhood

    *   Sin management and spiritual behavioral modification is not a fun home to grow up in if you're the kid.

3. ___*Grace*___ –Based Fatherhood

    *   God is a parent. ... He is parenting us.

    *   God is a God of ___*grace*___.

[1] Mueller, Carol M. *The Quotable John Wayne: The Grit and Wisdom of an American Icon* (New York. Taylor Trade Publishing. 2007)

"As each has received a gift, use it to serve one another, as good stewards of God's varied grace: whoever speaks, as one who speaks oracles of God; whoever serves, as one who serves by the strength that God supplies—in order that in everything God may be glorified through Jesus Christ. To him belong glory and dominion forever and ever. Amen."

1 Peter 4:10-11 (ESV)

"And God is able to make all grace abound to you, so that having all sufficiency in all things at all times, you may abound in every good work."

2 Corinthians 9:8 (ESV)

- Grace based parenting is simply treating your kids the way **God** treats you.

III. A GRACE BASED DAD

1. A grace based dad gives his kids the freedom to be **different**.

- Be careful of trying to make moral or biblical issues out of your arbitrary preferences.

- Everything changes when we let God's **grace** take over.

2. A grace based dad gives his kids the freedom to be **vulnerable**.

- We want to create a home where our kids don't have to wear a **masks**.

Grace Based Parenting - Book

- Our homes need to be a safe place for our kids to work through all the dangerous and fragile stuff of their lives.

"Let your speech always be gracious, seasoned with salt, so that you may know how you ought to answer each person."
Colossians 4:6 (ESV)

3. A grace based dad gives his kids the freedom to be ___candid___.

"Let us then with confidence draw near to the throne of grace, that we may receive mercy and find grace to help in time of need."
Hebrews 4:16 (ESV)

"Let all bitterness and wrath and anger and clamor and slander be put away from you, along with all malice."
Ephesians 4:31 (ESV)

- If we are just trying to control our kids, we ___deflate___ them, but when we keep them under control everything changes.

"See to it that no one fails to obtain the grace of God; that no 'root of bitterness' springs up and causes trouble, and by it many become defiled."
Hebrews 12:15 (ESV)

- The best way to make sure that they speak _respectfully_ to us is to speak respectfully to them.

4. A grace based dad gives his kids the freedom to make _mistakes_.

- Home must be a place where disappointments are tolerated and where hurts are endured and where mistakes never mean the end of a relationship.

> "My son, do not regard lightly the discipline of the Lord, nor be weary when reproved by him. For the Lord disciplines the one he loves, and chastises every son whom he receives."
>
> Hebrews 12:5-6 (ESV)

- Discipline and correction and boundaries are all forms of _grace_.

Jesus gives us the freedom to be different, vulnerable, candid and to make mistakes.

SESSION TWO | GRACE BASED

DISCUSSION / REFLECTION QUESTIONS

1. Tim says that "our heart connection to our kids is highly influenced by our heart connection with Jesus." Share what this looks like in your life.

2. Compare and contrast fear-based, performance-based, and grace-based fatherhood. Which of these is your natural tendency?

3. Tim shares four different kinds of freedom that grace based dads offer to their kids. Which of these do you find the most difficult to offer to your kids?

RESOURCES ON THE FOLLOWING PAGES:

- Grace Insights (p. 36-37)

- Grace Based Fatherhood (p. 38-41)

- THE RED ZONE: First Things First (p. 42-43)

GRACE INSIGHTS

BY DR. TIM KIMMEL

AS DAD, YOU'VE BEEN HANDED A PIECE OF HISTORY IN ADVANCE— **A GRACIOUS GIFT** YOU SEND TO A TIME YOU WILL NOT SEE.

FEAR-BASED FATHERHOOD IS **THE SUREST WAY** TO CREATE INTIMIDATED KIDS.

HIGH-CONTROL PARENTING HAPPENS WHEN WE **LEVERAGE THE STRENGTH OF OUR PERSONALITY AGAINST OUR CHILDREN'S WEAKNESS** TO GET THEM TO MEET OUR SELFISH AGENDA.

GRACE DOES NOT LOWER THE STANDARDS IN OUR HOMES, **IT RAISES THEM.**

EVERY CHILD'S THREE DRIVING INNER NEEDS:

1. A NEED FOR SECURITY
2. A NEED FOR SIGNIFICANCE
3. A NEED FOR STRENGTH

RULES NOT TEMPERED BY GRACE **BLOCK RELATIONSHIPS** WITH OUR CHILDREN AND LEAD TO REBELLION. ON THE OTHER SIDE, RELATIONSHIPS WITHOUT RULES **DON'T RESULT IN GRACE** EITHER.

GRACE BASED DADS AND THEIR FAMILIES ARE A BREATH OF FRESH AIR.

ALL QUOTES TAKEN FROM DR. TIM KIMMEL'S BOOK, *GRACE BASED PARENTING*

Kimmel, Grace Based Parenting: Set Your Family Free (Nashville, Thomas Nelson, 2004), 3, 12, 14, 40, 25, 37, 19.

GRACE BASED FATHERHOOD

GRACE

BASED

BY DR. TIM KIMMEL

This excerpt is taken from Dr. Tim Kimmel's book, GRACE BASED PARENTING.[1]

I HAVE A DIFFICULT TIME KEEPING MUCH MORE THAN THREE OR FOUR THINGS STRAIGHT IN MY HEAD AT ANY GIVEN TIME. THAT'S WHY I WAS RELIEVED TO LEARN THAT GOD HASN'T MADE THIS CONCEPT OF PARENTING WITH GRACE THAT DIFFICULT.

There are **FOUR BASIC THINGS** you need to do to maintain a grace-based environment for your children. If you get these four things up and running, then parenting challenges seem to find natural and reasonable solutions.

These four items will become a filter system that enables you to process the day-to-day dilemmas that come with raising kids. They will help you discern how to deliver grace in any given moment.

When these four things are done with the ***THREE INNER NEEDS*** of a

secure love, a significant purpose, a strong hope,

as their target, kids experience God's grace in a balanced way. This fourfold delivery system makes it a lot easier to show your children ***how to find love, purpose, and hope in Jesus Christ.***

[1] Tim Kimmel. *Grace Based Parenting: Set Your Family Free* (Nashville: Thomas Nelson, 2004), 134–135.

Grace-Based families are homes where children are given:

1 FREEDOM TO BE DIFFERENT

2 FREEDOM TO BE VULNERABLE

3 FREEDOM TO BE CANDID

4 FREEDOM TO MAKE MISTAKES

There's nothing magical about this matrix since it's simply the sum of how God deals with us through his grace. He made us with a gnawing need for security, for significance, and for strength. He helps us meet our need for security by finding a significant purpose in him. He helps us meet our need for strength by finding a strong hope in Him. The way we sense his grace each day is through the grace he grants us to be different, by the grace he extends to us when we are vulnerable, by the grace he allows us when we are candid with him, and by the grace he pours over us when we make mistakes.

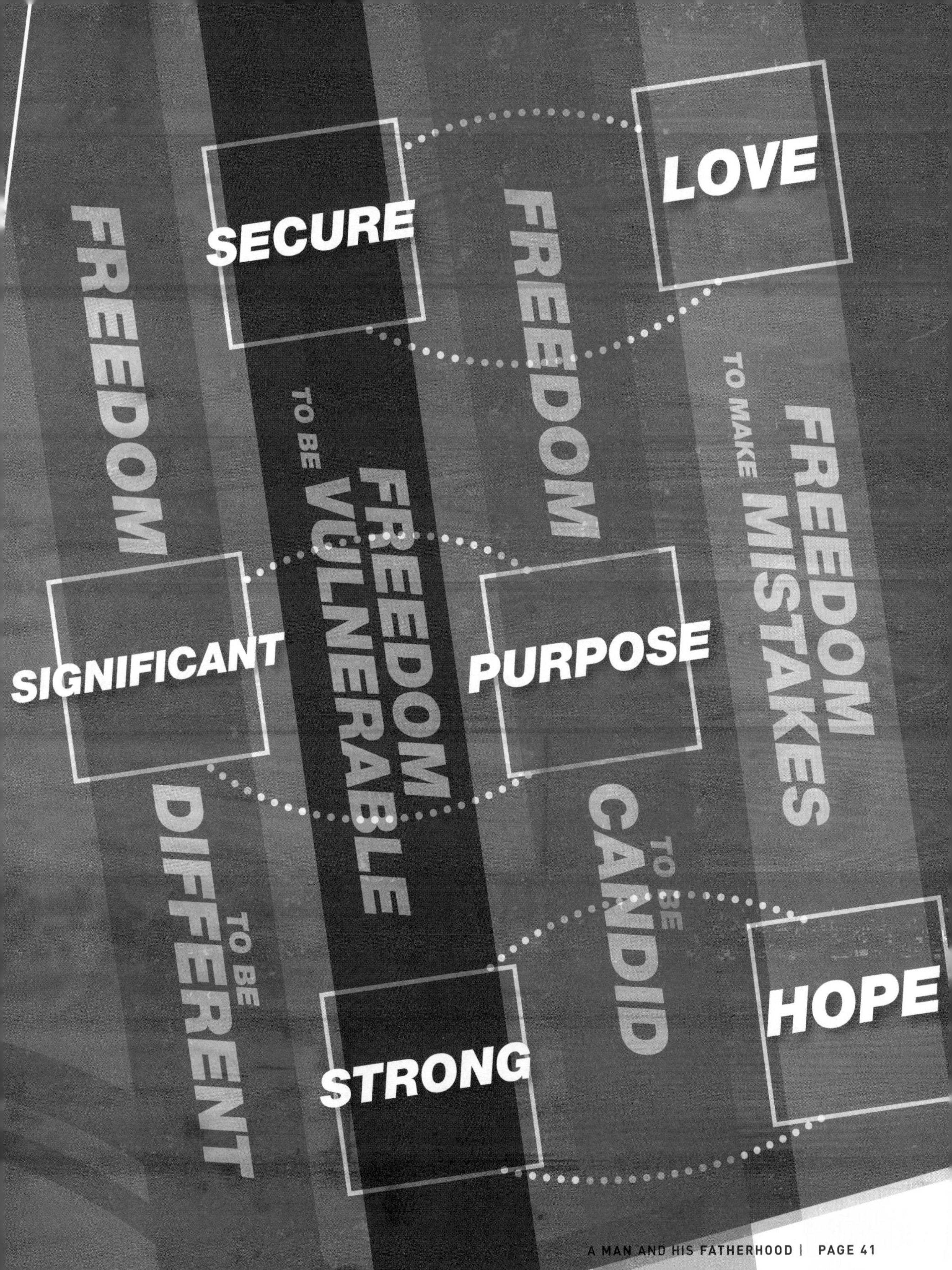

FREEDOM

SECURE

FREEDOM

LOVE

TO MAKE

FREEDOM
MISTAKES

TO BE

FREEDOM
VULNERABLE

SIGNIFICANT

PURPOSE

TO BE
CANDID

TO BE
DIFFERENT

HOPE

STRONG

1

FIRST THINGS FIRST

IN ORDER TO PARENT WITH GRACE, YOU MUST FIRST RECEIVE GOD'S GRACE FOR YOURSELF.

"LET US THEN WITH CONFIDENCE DRAW NEAR TO THE THRONE OF GRACE, THAT WE MAY RECEIVE MERCY AND FIND GRACE TO HELP IN TIME OF NEED."

HEBREWS 4:16

SCRIPTURE REFERENCES

1 Peter 4:10 (ESV) "As each has received a gift, use it to serve one another, as good stewards of God's varied grace."

2 Corinthians 9:8 (ESV) "And God is able to make all grace abound to you, so that having all sufficiency in all things at all times, you may abound in every good work."

Colossians 4:6 (ESV) "Let your speech always be gracious, seasoned with salt, so that you may know how you ought to answer each person."

Hebrews 4:16 (ESV) "Let us then with confidence draw near to the throne of grace, that we may receive mercy and find grace to help in time of need."

Ephesians 4:21 (ESV) "... assuming that you have heard about him and were taught in him, as the truth is in Jesus."

Hebrews 12:15 (ESV) "See to it that no one fails to obtain the grace of God; that no 'root of bitterness' springs up and causes trouble, and by it many become defiled.."

Hebrews 12:5-6 (ESV) "And have you forgotten the exhortation that addresses you as sons? 'My son, do not regard lightly the discipline of the Lord, nor be weary when reproved by him. For the Lord disciplines the one he loves, and chastises every son whom he receives.'"

The content in the resources above does not necessarily reflect that opinion of Authentic Manhood. Readers should utilize these resources but form their own opinions.

True Greatness

SESSION THREE | Training Guide

Training Guide OUTLINE

True Greatness Presented by Tim Kimmel

I. INTRODUCTION

1. If you chase the goals of the world, it is so easy to get off _____.

2. Most parents have a tendency to aim their children at a future focused on success.

3. It's so easy to take very legitimate parts of a child's life and over-prioritize them.

4. We can sabotage our children's future when we make _____ the goal of their future rather than an outcome of living a truly great life.

> "Do not love the world or the things in the world. If anyone loves the world, the love of the Father is not in him. For all that is in the world - the desires of the flesh and the desires of the eyes and pride of life - is not from the Father but is from the world. And the world is passing away along with its desires, but whoever does the will of God abides forever."
>
> 1 John 2:15-17 (ESV)

5. If we aim our children at wealth, beauty, power, and fame, we set them up for an adulthood that is _____.

II. DEFINING TRUE GREATNESS

True Greatness: a passionate love for Jesus Christ that shows itself in an unquenchable love and concern for _____.

> "I appeal to you therefore, brothers, by the mercies of God, to present your bodies as a living sacrifice, holy and acceptable to God, which is your spiritual worship. Do not be conformed to this world, but be transformed by the renewal of your mind, that by testing you may discern what is the will of God, what is good and acceptable and perfect."
>
> Romans 12:1-2 (ESV)

- Learning to live a life of true greatness sends children into the world focused upwards toward God and outwards toward others.

> "Set your minds on things that are above, not on things that are on earth."
>
> Colossians 3:2 (ESV)

III. FOUR QUALITIES OF TRUE GREATNESS:

1. A _____ Heart

   - A reverence for God and respect for others

   > "Do nothing from selfish ambition or conceit, but in humility count others more significant than yourselves. Let each of you look not only to his own interests, but also to the interests of others."
   >
   > Philippians 2:3-4 (ESV)

   > "God opposes, the proud but gives grace to the humble."
   >
   > James 4:6 (ESV)

2. A _____ Heart

- An appreciation for what they have been given and Who has given it to them

"Give thanks in all circumstances; for this is the will of God in Christ Jesus for you."

1 Thessalonians 5:18 (ESV)

3. A_____ Heart

- Taking a great delight in sharing with others what God has entrusted to you

"Give, and it will be given to you. Good measure, pressed down, shaken together, running over, will be put into your lap. For with the measure you use it will be measured back to you."

Luke 6:38 (ESV)

4. A_____Heart

- A willingness to take action in order to help someone else

IV. HOW TO INSTILL TRUE GREATNESS IN OUR KIDS

1. Be _____ of true greatness to your kids.

2. True greatness becomes the expectation in your home rather than the exception.

3. Provide _____ for your children to experience the lifestyle of true greatness.

. Valuing and praising our children's efforts at true greatness.

. PREPARING YOUR KIDS TO ANSWER THE THREE BIGGEST QUESTIONS IN LIFE

. What is my _____ going to be?

> "And whatever you do, in word or deed, do everything in the name
> of the Lord Jesus, giving thanks to God the Father through him. "
> Colossians 3:17 (ESV)

- A commitment to true greatness frees your children up to pursue
_____ plan for their lives rather than the world's.

. Who is my_____ going to be?

. Who is my_____ going to be?

> "If you aim at heaven you'll get earth thrown in, but you aim at earth and
> you'll get neither."
> - C.S. Lewis, *Mere Christianity* [1]

C.S. Lewis, *Mere Christianity* (1952; Harper Collins 2001) 134.

DISCUSSION / REFLECTION QUESTIONS

1. Are you pointing your kids towards worldly success or true greatness as defined by Tim? Discuss if it's easy to settle for success rather than true greatness.

2. Which of the four qualities of true greatness that Tim discussed is the most challenging for you to impart to your kids and why?

3. Share whether and how you are being an example of true greatness to your kids and then discuss some steps you can take to better model these qualities.

RESOURCES ON THE FOLLOWING PAGES:

TRUE GREA

True Greatness is a passionate love for God that demonstrates itself in an unquenchable love and concern for others.

GOD HAS MUCH BIGGER AND BETTER PLANS FOR OUR CHILDREN THAN MERELY INDULGING THEM.

We simply have to show our kids what true greatness looks like with our lives.

THE GREATEST REWARDS THAT EARTH HAS TO OFFER PALE IN COMPARISON TO THE MINIMUM THAT A LIFE OF TRUE GREATNESS HAS TO GIVE.

If you aim your children at anything less than greatness, you'll set them up to miss the whole point of their lives.

TRUE GREATNESS DOES NOT HAVE POWER AS ITS GOAL, BUT IT OFTEN GAINS POWER BY DEFAULT.

God has not called us to raise safe kids, He has called us to raise strong ones

GRACE IS THE PHENOMENAL POWER BEHIND TRUE GREATNESS.

TNESS

BY TIM KIMMEL

*QUOTES TAKEN FROM DR. TIM KIMMEL'S BOOK,
RAISING KIDS FOR TRUE GREATNESS.[1]

[1] Tim Kimmel, Raising Kids for True Greatness:
Redefine Success for You and Your Child
(Nashville: Thomas Nelson, 2006), P. 3,5,7,14,72, 73

a taste of

TRUE
GREATN

DR. TIM KIMMEL

ESS

This excerpt is taken from Dr. Tim Kimmel's Book,
Raisng Kids for True Greatness. [1]

It's really quite simple. Our kids are going to end up some-where. And we are going to aim them at something. Why not greatness?

When you think of the alternatives, none seem worthy of kids brought up in the shadow of the cross. We all want our kids to grow up to embody a passionate love for God that shows itself in a unquenchable love and concern for others.

WHEN IT COMES DOWN TO THE HONEST FEELINGS WITHIN OUR HEARTS THERE'S NO DEBATE - JUST ONE QUESTION...

CAN I DO IT?

[1] Tim Kimmel, Raising Kids for True Greatness: Redefine Success for You and Your Child (Nashville: Thomas Nelson, 2006), 197-199.

Can I, the person whose love for my children is second only to the God who created them and bought them on a cross, make the grade?

What's the matter? Are you thinking about those feet of clay you put your shoes over today? Don't worry about that;

GOD HAS BEEN USING THE WEAK TO CONFOUND THE WISE SINCE THE BEGINNING OF TIME.

What about those regrets? You've got them stuffed in bags and suitcases that clutter the hallways and back rooms of your heart. How about once and for all lugging them to the foot of the cross, dumping them out, and letting Jesus dispose of them for good?

"But I'm still weighed down with inadequacies," you may protest. "My knowledge is limited, my experiences are flawed, and I can't seem to get a grip on those fears that lurk in the corners of my conscience."

I'd like to say, " Get in line ... behind me and everyone else," but that doesn't address your legitimate concerns.

All I know is that God has been drawing straight lines with crooked sticks ever since the thief who hung next to him on the cross said, " Remember me when you come into your kingdom" (Luke 23:42)

Besides, raising kids for greatness is far less about what you do and far more about who you are. Moms and dads who decide to embody greatness are all a child really requires.

OUR KIDS JUST NEED AN IDEA OF WHAT GREATNESS LOOKS LIKE, FEELS LIKE, TASTES LIKE, SMELLS LIKE, AND SOUNDS LIKE.

AND ALL YOU HAVE TO DO GIVE YOUR CHILDREN THIS FIVE-SENSE VERSION OF GREATNESS IS REMEMBER ONE THING:

GRACE.

That's all this message is about. It's about taking the grace that God has given you and letting it permeate the pores of your life.

Let it seep through your intellect, volition, emotions, and spirit. Let its humility gratefulness, generosity, and servant attitude be the posture of your body, the position of your arms, and the constant expression on your face. When your kids experience God's grace through you on a daily basis, then grooming them for greatness will be easy. God did a great forgiveness for you. He did a great transformation in you. And he wants to do a great work through you. Let him do it. Give him the attitude, and let him squeeze out all the self, confusion, second-guessing, and fear... just let him wring it out of you. In its place, let the attitude of a great parent sine in everything you do. 🖪

A I M I N G
K I D S

AIMING OUR KIDS AT TRUE GREATNESS WITHIN AN ATMOSPHERE OF A GRACE-FILLED HOME BRINGS THE BEST OUT IN THEM.

EXCERPT FROM DR. TIM KIMMEL'S BOOK, *RAISING KIDS FOR TRUE GREATNESS*[1]

IT CURBS SIBLING RIVALRY

IT EMPOWERS KIDS TO FOCUS BETTER IN SCHOOL

IT INCLINES THEM TOWARD BETTER FRIENDS

IT PREPARES THEM TO DEAL WITH DIFFICULT PEOPLE

IT GIVES CHILDREN MORE RESPECT FOR LEADERSHIP AND AUTHORITY

IT HELPS KIDS RESPOND MORE POSITIVELY TO CORRECTION

IT SETS THEM UP TO BE GREATER ASSETS TO THE FUTURE

[1] Tim Kimmel, *Raising Kids for True Greatness: Redefine Success for You and Your Child* (Nashville: Thomas Nelson, 2006

the RED ZONE

TRUE
...GREATNESS

SCRIPTURE REFERENCES

1 John 2:15-17 (ESV) "Do not love the world or the things in the world. If anyone loves the world, the love of the Father is not in him. For all that is in the world—the desires of the flesh and the desires of the eyes and pride of life—is not from the Father but is from the world. And the world is passing away along with its desires, but whoever does the will of God abides forever."

Romans 12:1-2 (ESV) "I appeal to you therefore, brothers, by the mercies of God, to present your bodies as a living sacrifice, holy and acceptable to God, which is your spiritual worship. Do not be conformed to this world, but be transformed by the renewal of your mind, that by testing you may discern what is the will of God, what is good and acceptable and perfect."

Colossians 3:2 (ESV) "Set your minds on things that are above, not on things that are on earth."

Philippians 2:3-4 (ESV) "Do nothing from selfish ambition or conceit, but in humility count others more significant than yourselves. Let each of you look not only to his own interests, but also to the interests of others…"

James 4:6 (ESV) " But he gives more grace. Therefore it says, 'God opposes the proud, but gives grace to the humble.'"

1 Thessalonians 5:18 (ESV) "Give thanks in all circumstances; for this is the will of God in Christ Jesus for you."

Luke 6:38 (ESV) "Give, and it will be given to you. Good measure, pressed down, shaken together, running over, will be put into your lap. For with the measure you use it will be measured back to you."

Colossians 3:17 (ESV) "And whatever you do, in word or deed, do everything in the name of the Lord Jesus, giving thanks to God the Father through him."

Sons

SESSION FOUR | Training Guide

Sons
Presented by David Thomas & Stephen James

I. INTRODUCTION

How a man _____nurtures_____ a boy directly affects who he will grow into as a man.

Fathering a son is much more akin to _____growing_____ a tree than it is to constructing a building.

There is a _____framework_____ we can use when it comes to nurturing our sons.

II. FRAMEWORK FOR FATHERING SONS

1. _____Understanding_____

   • We've identified five stages of boyhood:

   The Explorer (ages 2-4)
   The Lover (ages 5-8)
   The Individual (ages 9-12)
   The Wanderer (ages 13-17)
   The Warrior (ages 18-22)

   • One common mistake is using the wrong things at the wrong ages.

   • A father also needs to have an awareness of his son's _____temperment_____.

2. _____Engaging_____

I. Without a dad _____engaged_____ in his story with him, a boy will get stuck left wondering if he has what it takes.

Explorer (ages 2-4)

- Boys need to experience the tender _____side_____ of masculinity.

- Explorer boys also need to _____wrestle_____.

Lover (ages 5-8)

- The focus needs to be more on _____enjoyment_____ than competition.

- A dad can teach a son to connect with his _____heart_____.

The Individual (ages 9–12)

- It's a dad's job to call out a son's _____strength_____.

- One thing dads need to look for is emotional vulnerability.

The Wanderer (ages 13–17)

- One way to stay engaged is by supporting all of his _____pursuits_____.

- Be careful to not care more about any activity in a son's life than the son does himself.

The Warrior (ages 18–22)

- Relationship in this stage is more about _____quality_____ than quantity.

- We need to make the transition to _____consultant_____.

3. __Validation__

- To validate him well means we need to do three things:

    1) Seeing Him

        - Having an appreciation for who he is

        - Maintaining a curiosity about who he is

        - Casting a vision for who he will become

    2) Naming Him

        - Has to do with the authority that we as dad have been given to speak truth into his life

    3) Drawing Him Out

        - Directed toward authenticity, integrity, and intimacy

4. __Initiating__ and __Cermony__

- Initiation is ~~foun~~ __Fundamental__ to the heart of a boy.

- It's more about revealing God's character.

- Boys need to be __celebrated__.

III. CONCLUSION

1. Understanding, Engaging, Validating, and Initiating

- A dad must first be _____present_____ in his own story.

- Every father needs:

    - a deep connection to the God who created him.

    - a bold vision for his own life.

    - a humbling participation greater than himself.

We have in us the _____power_____ to bless and the power to curse.

DISCUSSION / REFLECTION QUESTIONS

1. What insights did you gain from Stephen's and David's FRAMEWORK for raising sons?

2. Discuss whether and how you are living vicariously through your son's life and maybe caring more about some of his activities than he does. What or how should you consider changing?

3. Discuss the ways that your parenting is a blessing to your son(s). Share the areas that you may be wounding your son(s).

RESOURCES ON THE FOLLOWING PAGES:

- Seeing Your Son (p. 68-69)

- Engaging The Stages of Boyhood (p. 70-73)

- THE RED ZONE: A Dad's Prayer for His Son (p. 74-75)

TO LOVE A BOY WELL, we must become a student of him. To see him, we must observe him, consider him, perceive him, and learn him. This involves a lot of listening, patience, and attentiveness. The nature of seeing combines three elements:

1 A **CURIOSITY** ABOUT WHO HE IS

2 AN **APPRECIATION** FOR WHO HE IS

3 A **VISION** FOR WHO HE WILL BECOME

SEEING YOUR SON

BY STEPHEN JAMES AND DAVID THOMAS
EXCERPT FROM WILD THINGS: THE ART OF NURTURING BOYS [1]

[1] Stephen James and David Thomas, *Wild Things: The Art of Nurturing Boys* (Carol Stream, IL: Tyndale House, 2009), 199-201.

We don't need to keep a scientific log on our boys, but we do need to pay attention to the mundane details of their lives. We need to listen well to what's said and not said. We need to linger with them long enough to study them and to hear what they're not saying as well. We need to watch them when they interact with their peers and gather feedback from other adults who care for them.

You need to see how your boy is uniquely made—both the good and the bad, the strengths and the weaknesses, the interests and disinterests. Imagine where these characteristics will take him if they are not developed or refined. To see your boy is to also have a vision of who he is becoming and where he may end up if he follows the way of his heart. Having a vision helps us to structure a boy's life according to his design. Boys are so full of life that it's hard to know what to do with them sometimes. However, when we have a vision of who they are and who they are becoming we can engage with them and lead them toward the path they are to follow in their lives.

THE VISION WE HOLD FOR OUR BOYS BECOMES THE COMPASS THAT KEEPS THEM ON TRACK.

WE NEED TO BE CURIOUS ABOUT WHAT MAKES THEM TICK. HERE ARE SOME "SEEING" QUESTIONS TO ASK YOURSELF ABOUT YOUR BOY:

- What does he love to do?
- What is he afraid of?
- With whom does he spend time, and whom does he avoid?
- What is he like when you're not around?
- How does he perform for coaches and teachers?
- What is his favorite cereal?
- Who are his three best friends?
- Who is his favorite comic book hero, and why?
- When he is disappointed, what does he do?
- How well can he celebrate his own victories? What about the victories of others?
- Is he empathetic?
- What are his favorite, and least favorite, television shows, types of cars and music?
- What state or country does he want to visit?
- What really makes him mad?
- How does he hold his pencil?
- What does he like on his pizza?
- How does he relate to God?

ENGAGING THE
STAGES
OF
BOY
HOOD

IN EACH STAGE OF HIS JOURNEY, A BOY NEEDS HIS FATHER TO ENGAGE DIFFERENTLY.

THE EXPLORER
AGES 2-4

> NEED TO FEEL A MAN'S PHYSICAL PRESENCE: HUGS, KISSES, AND CUDDLES FOR LONG PERIODS OF TIME

> BOYS NEED TO EXPERIENCE THE TENDER SIDE OF MASCULINITY

> PHYSICAL INTERACTION BUILDS A SENSE OF SAFETY, SECURITY, AND COMFORT

> NEED TO WRESTLE, SO THEY CAN BEGIN TO FEEL AND TEST THEIR EMERGING STRENGTH

> NEED TO FEEL HIS FATHER'S STRENGTH IN THE SUPPORT OF HIS MOTHER

THE LOVER
AGES 5-8

> TO ENGAGE THE LOVER MEANS TO PAY CLOSE ATTENTION

> A BOY'S PERSONALITY WILL EMERGE, AND HE NEEDS HIS DAD TO IDENTIFY IT AND EXPLORE IT WITH HIM

> BOYS NEED TO BE EXPOSED TO A WIDE RANGE OF EXPERIENCES—INDOORS AND OUT

> THE FOCUS NEEDS TO BE MORE ON ENJOYMENT NOT COMPETITION

> THIS DOESN'T MEAN BOYS CAN'T COMPETE

> THE KEY WORD FOR KIDS THIS AGE IS FUN—NOT WIN

> LOVERS NEED PHYSICAL CONNECTION WITH DAD, BUT THEY ALSO NEED TO FEEL THEIR FATHER'S EMOTIONAL PRESENCE

THE INDIVIDUAL
AGES 9-12

> FOR A DAD TO ENGAGE THE INDIVIDUAL WELL YOU WILL NEED TO EXPAND YOUR REPERTOIRE

> BOYS AT THIS AGE NEED TO KNOW THEY ARE A FORCE TO BE RECKONED WITH

> IT'S YOU JOB AS A FATHER, TO CALL OUT YOUR SON'S STRENGT PHYSICAL AND EMOTIONAL

> HE NEEDS TO KNOW YOU SEE HIS STRENGTHS AND VALUE THEN

> RECOGNIZE AND AFFIRM HIS WILLINGNESS TO BE HONEST ABOUT HIS OWN WEAKNESSES AND STRUGGLES

THE WANDERER
AGES 13-17

➤ BOYS AT THIS STAGE ARE MAKING A SHIFT AWAY FROM PARENTS AND TOWARD FRIENDS AS THE PRIMARY INFLUENCE IN THEIR LIVES

➤ ONE WAY TO STAY ENGAGED IS BY SUPPORTING HIM IN HIS PURSUITS—WHETHER THEY ARE YOUR INTERESTS OR NOT

➤ YOU NEED TO BE CAREFUL TO NOT CARE MORE ABOUT ANY ACTIVITY OR INTEREST IN YOUR SON'S LIFE THAN THE SON DOES HIMSELF

➤ HELP HIM FIND TRUSTWORTHY MEN (COACHES, YOUTH PASTORS, TEACHERS) AND ENCOURAGE THESE RELATIONSHIPS

THE WARRIOR
AGES 18-22

➤ RELATIONSHIP IN THIS STAGE IS MORE ABOUT QUALITY THAN QUANTITY

➤ BOYS IN THE WARRIOR STAGE ARE FULL OF PROMISE, PURPOSE, INNOCENCE, AND INSIGHT

➤ HE'S READY TO FIGHT BUT LARGELY UNTESTED

➤ AS A FATHER YOU CAN'T GO TO BATTLE FOR HIM (THOUGH SOME OF US WILL TRY)

➤ YOU, AS DAD, TRANSITION TO CONSULTANT AND COMRADE

➤ HE IS TRYING TO FIGURE OUT WHAT IT MEANS FOR HIM TO BE A MAN, YOUR JOB AS DAD IS TO FIND WAYS TO FIT YOURSELF INTO HIS LIFE

GENERAL DOUGLAS MACARTHUR PENNED THIS PRAYER FOR HIS ONLY SON, ARTHUR, WHILE STATIONED IN AUSTRALIA:

Build me a son, O Lord, who will be strong enough to know when he is weak and brave enough to face himself when he is afraid; one who will be proud and unbending in honest defeat, and humble and gentle in victory.

Build me a son whose wishes will not take the place of deeds; a son who will know Thee—and that to know himself is the foundation stone of knowledge.

Lead him, I pray, not in the path of ease and comfort, but under the stress and spur of difficulties and challenge. Here let him learn to stand up in the storm; here let him learn compassion for those who fail.

Build me a son whose heart will be clear, whose goal will be high; a son who will master himself before he seeks to master other men; one who will reach into the future, yet never forget the past.

And after all these things are his, add, I pray, enough of a sense of humor, so that he may always be serious, yet never take himself too seriously. Give him humility, so that he may always remember the simplicity of true greatness, the open mind of true wisdom, and the weakness of true strength.

Then I, his father will dare to whisper, "I have not lived in vain."

[1] **Bennet, William J.** *The Book of Man* (Nashville: Thomas Nelson, 2011) page. 413–414

A DAD'S PRAYER FOR HIS SON

SESSION FOUR | SONS

SUPPORTING RESOURCES

James, Stephen. Thomas, David. J. *Wild Things-The Art of Nurturing Boys.* Carol Stream, Il. Tyndale 2009.

Daughters

SESSION FIVE | Training Guide

Daughters Presented by Dr. Meg Meeker

I. STRONG FATHERS, STRONG DAUGHTERS

1. You are the most _____**most**_____ man in your daughter's life.

    • You are your daughter's first exposure to male love.

2. She knows you're _____**different**_____ than her mother.

3. What is your daughter looking for?

    • if you're going to keep her safe
    • if she's ok around you
    • if you're going to go away and never come back
    • if she can trust what you have to give her

4. Set her on a course of having _____**solid**_____ relationships with men.

    • You set a _____**template**_____ over her heart for how she will relate to men.

5. She is going to be much more open to a relationship with God later in life.

    • You leave an _____**impact**_____ on her soul and on her life.

6. It's never to late to regroup with your daughter.

    • You can't talk to your daughters the way you talk to your sons.

    • What your daughter wants from you is just for you to _____~~taste~~ **listen**_____ to her.

- Be very careful in the _____words_____ that you use with her.

- The words you speak in your daily lives _____change_____ who your daughter becomes.

- Your daughter's identity is _____shaped_____ by reading you.

7. It is important for dads to teach their daughters about _____faith_____.

8. Teach your daughters to _____fight_____.

9. The most important thing you can do is give her physical _____affection_____.

- Never take it _____personally_____.

- What she is really is saying is "Dad, am I worth fighting for?"

- If you engage your daughter, that's the best protection she can have.

DISCUSSION / REFLECTION QUESTIONS

1. Discuss how knowing that you're the most important man in your daughter's life makes you feel as Dad.

2. Share how well you're doing giving physical affection to your daughter. If you've ever experienced the resistence that Meg referred to, how have you handled that?

3. Would your daughter say that you listen to her well? What are some things you can do to let her know you're listening and that you care about what she is saying?

4. What is your main take-away from this session on loving your daughter well?

RESOURCES ON THE FOLLOWING PAGES:

- Connecting to The Heart (p. 82-83)

- Dads, Your Daughters Need You (p. 84-87)

- THE RED ZONE: Some Great Daddy Daughter Movies
        (p. 88-89)

Connecting

TO THE

HEART

BY TIERCE GREEN

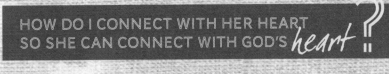

HOW DO I CONNECT WITH HER HEART SO SHE CAN CONNECT WITH GOD'S *heart*?

That question drives me the most as I stand at the plate ready to swing away at being a good father for my daughter. No pressure, but she's an only child—I don't get a do-over if I screw this up! Here are three things that help me keep my eye on the ball and connect with her heart:

1 DIE TO LIVE

We cover this principle in Volume 5 of 33 as it relates to a man and his marriage. The same principle applies to fatherhood. As a dad, the moment I begin to think "I've got this" is when things start to unravel. In Luke 9:23-24 (ESV) Jesus told His followers: "If anyone would come after me, let him deny himself and take up his cross daily and follow me. For whoever would save his life will lose it, but whoever loses his life for my sake will save it."

In dying to myself, I must not go soft and drift into passivity, but in accepting responsibility and leading courageously I must not grow harsh either. I need to be authoritative without becoming an authoritarian. Fatherhood must reflect servant leadership.

2 REST IN GOD'S GRACE

Just about every day we pray as a family, "God, help us see others the way you see them. Help us extend grace to others as you have extended grace to us." That prayer reflects what Jesus said in Luke 6:36 (ESV): "Be merciful, just as your Father is merciful."

Remembering what God has done for me is a game-changer as a dad. It helps me focus on my daughter's heart and her need for Jesus, not just my need for her behavior to change. When she was only four-years-old, I gave her a tiny silver ring with a heart on it and promised that God will love her no matter what, and so will I.

3 VULNER-ABILITY

I don't hesitate to draw a hard line when necessary, but one night I crossed the line into harsh leadership. After the fact, I knew I needed to clean up my mess. Kneeling beside her bed before we prayed that night, I opened my heart: "What I said to you earlier was right, but the way I said it was really wrong. I need to ask you to forgive me."

In another instance, I was trying to help her face her fears about some things. It felt like I was taking a big chance when I said to her, "Anna, I've never told you this, but before you were born, when I was thinking about the responsibility of being a father, I was so afraid that I wouldn't be a good dad for you. I asked God to help me then and every day since ... and He has. I know God will help you with your fears like He is helping me." Taking the risk of being vulnerable with her opened up a much deeper and honest conversation.

Successful fatherhood isn't batting 1000. None of us are going to be perfect dads. But if we'll die to live, rest in God's grace and be willing to be vulnerable, we'll be much closer to connecting with her heart. 33

Dads, your daughters need you.

BY DR. MEG MEEKER

AUTHOR *STRONG FATHERS, STRONG DAUGHTERS*

MEN,

we need you.

We—mothers, daughters, and sisters—need your help to raise healthy young women. We need every ounce of masculine courage and wit you own, **because fathers, more than anyone else, set the course for a daughter's life.**

Your daughter needs the best of who you are: your strength, your courage, your intelligence, and your fearlessness. She needs your empathy, assertiveness, and self-confidence. She needs you.

Our daughters need the support that only fathers can provide—and if you are willing to guide your daughter, to stand between her and a toxic culture, to take her to a healthier place, your rewards will be unmatched. You will experience the love and adoration that can come only from a daughter. You will feel a pride, satisfaction, and joy that you can know nowhere else.

After more than twenty years of listening to daughters—and doling out antibiotics, anti-depressants, and stimulants to girls who have gone without a father's love—I know just how important fathers are. I have listened hour after hour to young girls describe how they vomit in junior high bathrooms to keep their weight down. I have listened to fourteen-year-old girls tell me they have to provide oral sex—which disgusts them—in order to keep their boyfriends. I've watched girls drop off varsity tennis teams, flunk out of school, and carve initials or tattoo cult figures onto their bodies—all to see if their dads will notice.

And I have watched daughters talk to fathers. When you come in the room, they change. Everything about them changes: their eyes, their mouths, their gestures, their body language. Daughters are never lukewarm in the presence of their fathers. They might take their mothers for granted, but not you. They light up—or they cry. They watch you intensely. They hang on your words. They hope for your attention, and they wait for it in frustration—or in despair. They need a gesture of approval, a nod of encouragement, or even simple eye contact to let them know you care and are willing to help.

When she's in your company, your daughter tries harder to excel. When you teach her, she learns more rapidly. When you guide her, she gains confidence.

If you fully understood just how profoundly you can influence your daughter's life, you would be overwhelmed.

Boyfriends, brothers, even husbands can't shape her character the way you do. You will influence her entire life because she gives you an authority she gives no other man.

Many fathers (particularly of teen girls) assume they have little influence over their daughters—certainly less influence than their daughters' peers or pop culture—and think their daughters need to figure out life on their own. But your daughter faces a world markedly different from the one you did growing up: it's less friendly, morally unmoored, and even outright dangerous. After age six, "little girl" clothes are hard to find. Many outfits are cut to make her look like a seductive thirteen- or fourteen-year-old girl trying to attract older boys. She will enter puberty earlier than girls did a generation or two ago (and boys will be watching as she begins to physically mature even as young as age nine). She will see sexual innuendo or scenes of overt sexual behavior in magazines or on television before she is ten years old, whether you approve or not. She will learn about HIV and AIDS in elementary school and will also probably learn why and how it is transmitted.

If you're reading this, you are a motivated, sensitive, and caring father. You are a good man, but you're probably exhausted. For you, there is great news and bad news.

The great news is that in order to experience a richer life and raise a fabulous daughter, you don't need to change your character. You need only to indulge what's best in your character. You have everything you need for a better relationship with your daughter.

Here's the bad news.

You need to stop in your tracks, open your eyes wider, and see what your daughter faces today, tomorrow, and in ten years. It's tough and it's frightening, but this is the way it is. While you want the world to be cautious and gentle with her, it is cruel beyond imagination—even before she is a teen. Even though she may not participate in ugly stuff, it's all around her: sexual promiscuity, alcohol abuse, foul language, illegal drugs, and predatory boys and men who want only to take something from her.

Don't think you can't fight her "peers" or the power of pop culture. Exactly the opposite is true. Yes, the four Ms—MTV, music, movies, and magazines—are enormous influences that shape what girls think about themselves, what clothes they wear, and even the grades they get. But their influence doesn't come close to the influence of a father. A lot of research has been done on this—and fathers always come out on top. The effects of loving, caring fathers on their daughters' lives can be measured in girls of all ages.

When you are with her, whether you eat dinner and do homework together or even when you are present but don't say much, the quality and stability of her life—and, you'll find, your own—improves immeasurably. Even if you think the two of you operate on different planes, even if you worry that time spent with her shows no measurable results, even if you doubt you are having a meaningful impact on her, the clinical fact is that you are giving your daughter the greatest of gifts.

Your daughter will view this time spent with you vastly differently than you do. Over the years, in erratic bursts and in simple ordinary life together, she will absorb your influence. She will watch every move you make. She might not understand why you are happy or angry, affectionate, **but you will be the most important man in her life, forever.**

When she is twenty-five, she will mentally size her boyfriend or husband up against you. When she is thirty-five, the number of children she has will be affected by her life with you. The clothes she wears will reflect something about you. Even when she is seventy-five, how she faces her future will depend on some distant memory of time you spent together. Be it good or painful, the hours and years you spend with her—or don't spend with her—change who she is. **Come on men, we daughters need you!** 🧩

> **Fathers are what stand between daughters and this toxic world.**

SOME GREAT DADDY DAUGHTER

★ ★ ★ ★ ★ ★ ★ ★ ★ ★

MOVIES

the RED ZONE

FATHER OF THE BRIDE: PART 1 & 2

REMEMBER THE TITANS

THE PARENT TRAP

TROUBLE WITH THE CURVE

WE BOUGHT A ZOO

ENCHANTED

INSIDE OUT

BRAVE

THREE MEN AND A BABY

* BE SURE TO USE YOUR DISCRETION FOR AGE APPROPRIATENESS.

ADMIT ONE ★ ADMIT ONE ★ ADMIT ONE ★ ADMIT ONE ★ ADMIT ONE

ADMIT ONE ★ ADMIT ONE ★ ADMIT ONE ★ ADMIT ONE ★ ADMIT ONE

THE SERIES

SESSION FIVE | DAUGHTERS

SUPPORTING RESOURCES

Meeker, Meg. *Strong Fathers, Strong Daughters.* New York. Ballantine Books, 2007.

* The content in the resources above does not necessarily reflect the opinion of Authentic Manhood.

Readers should utilize these resources but form their own opinions.

Decisions

SESSION SIX | Training Guide

Decisions Presented by Bryan Carter

I. INTRODUCTION

There is almost nothing more important in raising kids than parental _consistancy_.

II. DECISIONS

1. Technology

   - The new _reality_ is that we have instant access to technology.

   - Key Questions to ask:

     o How much screen-time are your kids allowed to have each day?
     o When and who gets a Facebook or social media account?
     o At what age can the kids have a smart phone?
     o Who's going to monitor your kid's texts and instant messaging?

   - Play _offense_ and lay some ground rules.

2. Friends

   - Healthy friendships are _beneficial_ to kids.

   - Friends can also be a negative influence.

     "Whoever walks with the wise becomes wise, but the companion of fools will suffer harm."

     Proverbs 13:20 (ESV)

- Key Questions to ask:

  o How much time are your kids allowed to spend with their friends?

  o With whom and how long are they allowed to stay out at night?

  o Where do you stand in regard to sleepovers?

  o Will your child be allowed to date?

- _____Equip_____ your kids to recognize worthy friends.

3. Schools

   - Many families will have a _____choice_____ as to where you send your kids' to school.

   - Reevaluate each of your kids' school needs each year.

   - School is NOT primarily _____responsible_____ for your kids' education.

4. Family Size

   - God ultimately decides whether, when, and how many in regards to the number of kids you will have .

   - Romans 8:28 says He works all things for _____good_____ for His children.

   - Family size should probably be an _____ongoing_____ conversation.

5. Family Time

   - Fight to have _____unrushed_____, unhurried quality time as a family.

- Key Questions to ask:

  o To what degree are you willing to allow your kids to be active outside the home?

  o Will you have a sit-down family meal most nights?

  o How many sports will your kids play?

- Create an environment of ___fun___.

- You will also want to make some decisions around the spiritual ___rhytms___ of your family.

6. Discipline

  - Discipline should be fair, age-appropriate, consistent, and restorative.

  - We must be careful not to ___over discipline___ our children or to discipline for the wrong reasons.

    "Fathers, do not provoke your children to anger by the way you treat them."

    Ephesians 6:4a (NLT)

7. Equipping Your Kids to Make Wise Decisions

    "The fear of the LORD is the beginning of wisdom..."

    Proverbs 9:10 (ESV)

  - The ___ultimate___ goal of parenting for the Authentic Man is to raise God-fearing, grace-depending, Jesus-following adults who will be a bright light.

"All things were created through him and for him. And he is before all things, and in him all things hold together."

Colossians 1:16–17 (ESV)

"Your word is a lamp to my feet and a light to my path."

Psalm 119:105 (ESV)

- Jesus died on the cross to offer us ___*grace*___ for when we fall short as fathers.

"Now may the God of peace—who brought up from the dead our Lord Jesus, the great Shepherd of the sheep, and ratified an eternal covenant with his blood—may he equip you with all you need for doing his will. May he produce in you, through the power of Jesus Christ, every good thing that is pleasing to him. All glory to him forever and ever! Amen."

Hebrews 13:20-21 (NLT)

SESSION SIX | DECISIONS

DISCUSSION / REFLECTION QUESTIONS

1. Discuss with your group any challenges your family faces with social media and technology. How are you managing social media and technology?

2. Have you ever struggled with over-disciplining or under-disciplining your kids? Evaluate if your discipline is fair, age-appropriate, consistent and restorative for your kids.

3. In what areas have you needed to show grace to your kids and what areas have you had to ask for grace from your kids?

4. Closing Challenge: Discuss what it would be like to create a community of men and to initate taking them through this material on fatherhood. Imagine the influence that would have on both them and their kids' (some of whom may be your own kids' friends!).

RESOURCES ON THE FOLLOWING PAGES:

I say this all the time: there are few things in life that rise to the same level of importance as fathering.

How significant is the calling upon fathers to be the primary instruments in the shaping of a human soul?

It's a calling that we should accept with humility and holy fear, but also with excitement and courage because Christ is with us and for us.

FAT
TR

But over the years, I've had thousands of conversations with Christian fathers who are discouraged, angry, grieved and ready to quit (or who have already quit). Thousands of fathers don't know what they're doing or why they're doing it. They've simply lost their way, or in many cases, they never knew the way to begin with.

Why is this? Well, there are several reasons I think, but I want to focus on just one:

we have fallen into the trap of believing that our calling is to enforce **LAW,** *when in fact God has chosen for us to restore* **AWE.**

E. PAUL TRIPP

Are rules important in parenting? Absolutely! Your family won't be able to function if every kid can do and say as they want. Is discipline necessary? Yes, the Proverbs are filled with reasons why. But, your fathering strategies must go deeper than setting up and enforcing rules. You must target the heart of your child.

Beneath the layers of their personality, **YOUR CHILD HAS A HEART HARDWIRED FOR AWE,** but sin has enabled their heart to wander from the Lord; you should know from personal experience! So, God has ordained for fathers to do everything we can to restore the awe of God *in the hearts of our children.*

HOW DO YOU DO THAT? LET ME GIVE YOU FOUR BRIEF EXAMPLES:

TALK
1

It's very easy for us to settle for superficial and insignificant chit-chat with our kids. Instead, locate heart-focused and gospel-centered talking points and engage. Talk about the significance of human relationships and how sin has the ability to destroy them. Talk about the reasons why we can and should love difficult siblings, neighbors, friends and classmates. Talk about personal identity and the reasons we find it in the world instead of in Christ.

SHOW
2

God created the physical world to reflect his magnificence and power. Take your kids to see their favorite animal at the zoo and gaze in wonder with them at its size and color. Take a day trip to a mountain or lake; go fishing; watch the sunset-and while you're there, remind your child that all of that creativity came out of the mind of God.

FOR MORE PAUL TRIPP RESOURCES ON PARENTING AND FATHERHOOD, VISIT WWW.PAULTRIPP.COM AND CONNECT ON FACEBOOK AT /PDTRIPP AND @PAULTRIPP ON TWITTER.

MIRROR 3

When your kids break God's law, treat them as God treats us. Mirror the tone of his voice; mirror the look on his face; mirror the nature of his character. Every time you exercise authority, it should mirror the patient, firm, gracious, wise, loving, tender, merciful, forgiving, and faithful authority of God.

SHARE 4

Finally, when your children struggle with sin, share how you struggle in the same way: "I get angry too when things don't go my way at work-I know how you feel and I often react in the same way." Or, "When people gossip behind my back, I want to spread nasty rumors about them, just like you." Don't pretend that you don't struggle like your kid. Share in their pain and sin and point them to the help and hope found in Christ.

I said at the beginning that we should approach fathering with humility and a holy fear. Why? Because you and I have no ability to talk, show, mirror, and share as we're called. Sin and selfishness hijack our best fathering intentions, and we'll respond with anger, impatience, and self-righteousness.

It's only when we live in awe of God and his glory and his grace that we'll be able to help our kids do the same. You can't give away what your heart already doesn't possess as a parent, so why don't you spend the next few minutes asking the Lord to restore his awe upon your soul.

Scott,

You know I'm not big into posting things on Facebook, but I wanted to post this letter from me to you for the world to see.

Well "Bubba," It'd be easy for me to sit here and write about how much I'm going to miss you and how it's not fair that I'm loosing the greatest uncle to ever live, but I'm not going to do that because you wouldn't want me to. **Instead, I'm going to tell you why/how you were one of the most influential men I've ever known.**

On the day I found out you were gone I drove back to Little Rock and went straight to your home. There were hundreds of people there doing whatever they could to help calm the storm and I was blown away. I quickly made my way upstairs to your office to have a moment alone. As I sat there crying, I began looking at all of the pictures of you, Mary, and the kids while trying to keep myself together.

Now you and I both know that you were never a sports junky by any means, which brings me to my first example of your amazing influence. I looked over on your desk and saw a piece of paper with instructions on how to hit a baseball. I lost it. You would be the first to admit that you weren't the most experienced coach in the land, but you did it anyway because you saw a greater opportunity other than winning the Cal Ripkin World Series. You saw an opportunity to influence young kids' lives and you were the best of the best at this. I mean, look at yourself in this picture. If someone who didn't know you saw this they would've thought you were a decendent of Vince Lombardi! This is why you had every bit of business being a coach. **This is what influence looks like.**

You know how I mentioned that there were hundreds of people at your house? Yeah, well that continued on for the next three days. You think people just didn't have anything else to do? No. They were there solely because of the impact you had on their lives and now your family will feel the love that you gave others for the rest of their lives. Did you know that Mary and the kids are 100% set on food for the next six months? That's a lot of food even for you Scott. People want to help your family and love on them because of the love and help you offered to them while you were here.

Oh by the way, did you know that certain people have generously offered to help fund your kids' college tuition, or that someone anonymously paid for your funeral? I promise you they're not doing it because they had no other use for their money, they're doing it because sometime/somewhere during your life you chose to care about them and make them feel special. **That is what influence looks like.**

Finally, your greatest influence is yet to come. That's right. I received dozens of texts following your funeral from people who "want to live their lives the way Scott Snider did" and I don't think they meant they want to be able to sing as well as you (although it'd be a great bonus). And I know you'd blush if I said this, but **a world with people waking up with the mentality of loving others the way Scott Snider loved others would be a pretty amazing world to live in.**

Now, I know this isn't goodbye but I promise to do my best to move on and live my life to the fullest because I know that's what you would've wanted. I love ya bubba and I can't wait to see you again.

Your loving nephew,

Jack

THE COACH
WHO KNEW A LITTLE ABOUT FOOTBALL
BUT EVERYTHING ABOUT
INFLUENCE

LOVE
BIG!

WORK
HARD!

SPEAK
HUMBLY!

PLAY
ENTHUSIASTICALLY!

FORGIVE
GLADLY!

REPENT
QUICKLY!

THINK
ABUNDANTLY!

AND...NEVER STOP
DANCING!

the RED ZONE

*Taken from *Raising Kids for True Greatness*
by Dr. Tim Kimmel[1]

[1] Tim Kimmel, *Raising Kids for True Greatness: Redefine
Success for You and Your Child* (Nashville: Thomas Nelson,

God, Marriage, and Family

By Andreas Köstenberger

*Köstenberger and Jones explore the latest contro-
versies, cultural shifts, and teachings within both
the church and society and further apply Scripture's
timeless principles to contemporary issues. Includes
an assessment of the family-integrated church movement; discussion of recent debates on corporal pun-
ishment, singleness, homosexuality, and divorce and
remarriage; new sections on the theology of sex and
the parenting of teens; and updated bibliographies.*

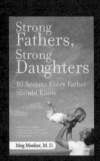

How Children Raise Parents: The Art of Listening to Your Children

By Dan Allender

*To reduce the pressure and enjoy greater closeness in your
family, turn your parenting upside-down by allowing God to
use your children to help you grow up. Imagine what would
happen if you began to prize what you're being taught by
your children's quirks, failures, and normal childhood dilemmas, rather than worrying about whether you're doing everything right as a parent. Now you can let go of the pressure to
make sure your children succeed, and instead learn to grow
into spiritual maturity by listening to your children.*

Boundaries with Kids: How Healthy Choices Grow Healthy Children By Henry Cloud

*Here is the help you need for raising your kids to take responsibility
for their actions, attitudes, and emotions. Drs. Henry Cloud and John
Townsend take you through the ins and outs of instilling the kind of
character in your children that will help them lead balanced, produc-
tive, and fulfilling adult lives.*

Bringing Up Boys

By James Dobson

*With so much confusion about the role of men in our society, it's no wonder
so many parents and teachers are asking questions about how to bring up
boys. Why are so many boys in crisis? What qualities should we be trying
to instill in young males? Our culture has vilified masculinity and, as a
result, an entire generation of boys is growing up without a clear idea of
what it means to be a man. In the runaway bestseller Bringing Up Boys,
Dr. Dobson draws from his experience as a child psychologist and family
counselor, as well as extensive research, to offer advice and encouragement based on a firm foundation of biblical principles.*

Strong Fathers, Strong Daughters

By Meg Meeker

*Dr. Meeker articulates that fathers are
far more powerful than many themselves
believe. Dr. Meeker also states that daughters need the support that only fathers
can provide – and if they are willing to
follow Dr. Meeker's advice and experience
on how to guide their daughters, to stand
between them and a toxic culture, their
rewards will be unmatched.*

Shepherding a Child's Heart

By Tedd Tripp

*Written for parents with children of any
age, this insightful book provides perspec-
tives and procedures for shepherding
your child's heart into the paths of life.
Shepherding a Child's Heart gives fresh
biblical approaches to child rearing.*

Bringing Up Girls

By James Dobson

*Peer pressure. Eating disorders. Decisions
about love, romance, and sex. Academic
demands. Life goals and how to achieve
them. These are just some of the challenges
that girls face today and the age at which
they encounter them is getting younger and
younger. As a parent, how are you guiding
your daughter on her journey to womanhood
Are you equipping her to make wise choices?
Whether she's still playing with dolls or in th
midst of the often-turbulent teen years, is she
truly secure in her identity as your valued an
loved daughter? In the New York Times bestseller Bringing Up Girls, Dr. James Dobson
will help you face the challenges of raising
your daughters to become strong, healthy, a
confident women who excel in life.*

RESOURCES

Ten Ways to Destroy the Imagination of Your Child

By Anthony Esolen

Play dates, soccer practice, day care, political correctness, drudgery without facts, television, video games, constant supervision, endless distractions: these and other insidious trends in child rearing and education are now the hallmarks of childhood. As author Anthony Esolen demonstrates in this elegantly written, often wickedly funny book, almost everything we are doing to children now constricts their imaginations, usually to serve the ulterior motives of the constrictors. Ten Ways to Destroy the Imagination of Your Child confronts contemporary trends in parenting and schooling by reclaiming lost traditions. This practical, insightful book is essential reading for any parent who cares about the paltry thing that childhood has become, and who wants to give a child something beyond the dull drone of today's culture.

True Greatness

By Tim Kimmel

You want only the best for your kids. And you want them to be successful. Sure, there's nothing wrong with that. But what if there was something more? Could your definition of success be leaving out the most important part?

What about greatness? Where does it fit in? "If you aim your children at anything less than greatness, you'll set them up to miss the whole point of their lives," says author Tim Kimmel. In Raising Kids for True Greatness, Kimmel turns the definition of success on its head and guides you in preparing your child for a life that will easily eclipse the goals of those who are merely successful.

Grace-Based Parenting

By Tim Kimmel

Rejecting rigid rules and checklists that don't work, Dr. Kimmel recommends a parenting style that mirrors God's love, reflects His forgiveness, and displaces fear as a motivator for behavior. As we embrace the grace God offers, we begin to give it-creating a solid foundation for growing morally strong and spiritually motivated children.

Raising a Modern-Day Knight

By Dr. Robert Lewis

What does it mean to be a man? Moreover, how does a father instill these qualities in his son? By Raising a Modern-Day Knight. Beginning with a biblical perspective of manhood, author-pastor Robert Lewis shares a unique approach to shaping a boy into a man by equipping him with three essential elements: a vision, a code of conduct, and a cause (Christianity) in which to invest his life. Complete with ceremony ideas to celebrate accomplishments and ingrain them in his mind, this softcover is as insightful as it is practical in raising a boy to be a chivalrous, godly man.

Wild Things: The Art of Nurturing Boys

By Stephen James and David Thomas

Playing off the themes in the Caldecott Medal-winning children's book Where the Wild Things Are, this informative, practical, and encouraging guide will help parents guide boys down the path to healthy and authentic manhood. Wild Things addresses the physical, emotional, and spiritual parts of a boy, written by two therapists who are currently engaged in clinical work with boys and their parents and who are also fathers raising five sons. Contains chapters such as "Sit Still! Pay Attention!" "Deficits and Disappointments," and "Rituals, Ceremonies, and Rites of Passage."

* The content in the resources recommended above does not necessarily reflect the opinion of Authentic Manhood. Readers should utilize these resources but form their own opinions.

THE WORD AND FATHERHOOD

Exodus 20:12 "Honor your father and your mother, that your days may be long in the land that the LORD your God is giving you."

Deuteronomy 4:9 "Only take care, and keep your soul diligently, lest you forget the things that your eyes have seen, and lest they depart from your heart all the days of your life. Make them known to your children and your children's children."

Deuteronomy 5:16 "Honor your father and your mother, as the LORD your God has commanded you, so that you may live long and that it may go well with you in the land the LORD your God is giving you."

Deuteronomy 6:6–9 "And these words that I command you today shall be on your heart. You shall teach them diligently to your children, and shall talk of them when you sit in your house, and when you walk by the way, and when you lie down, and when you rise. You shall bind them as a sign on your hand, and they shall be as frontlets between your eyes. You shall write them on the doorposts of your house and on your gates."

Deuteronomy 11:18–19 "You shall therefore lay up these words of mine in your heart and in your soul, and you shall bind them as a sign on your hand, and they shall be as frontlets between your eyes. You shall teach them to your children, talking of them when you are sitting in your house, and when you are walking by the way, and when you lie down, and when you rise.

Psalm 78:5 "He established a testimony in Jacob and appointed a law in Israel, which he commanded our fathers to teach to their children."

Psalm 127:3–5 "Behold, children are a heritage from the LORD, the fruit of the womb a reward. Like arrows in the hand of a warrior are the children of one's youth. Blessed is the man who fills his quiver with them! He shall not be put to shame when he speaks with his enemies in the gate."

Psalm 139:13–16 "For you formed my inward parts; you knitted me together in my mother's womb. I praise you, for I am fearfully and wonderfully made. Wonderful are your works; my soul knows it very well. My frame was not hidden from you, when I was being made in secret, intricately woven in the depths of the earth. Your eyes saw my unformed substance; in your book were written, every one of them, the days that were formed for me, when as yet there was none of them."

Proverbs 1:8–9 "Hear, my son, your father's instruction, and forsake not your mother's teaching, for they are a graceful garland for your head and pendants for your neck."

Proverbs 3:11–12 "My son, do not despise the LORD's discipline or be weary of his reproof, for the LORD reproves him whom he loves, as a father the son in whom he delights."

Proverbs 6:20 "My son, keep your father's commandment, and forsake not your mother's teaching."

Proverbs 10:1 "A wise son makes a glad father, but a foolish son is a sorrow to his mother."

Proverbs 13:24 "Whoever spares the rod hates his son, but he who loves him is diligent to discipline him."

Proverbs 14:26 "In the fear of the LORD one has strong confidence, and his children will have a refuge."

Proverbs 17:6 "Grandchildren are the crown of the aged, and the glory of children is their fathers."

Proverbs 20:7 "The righteous who walks in his integrity—blessed are his children after him!"

Proverbs 22:6 "Train up a child in the way he should go; even when he is old he will not depart from it."

Proverbs 22:15 "Folly is bound up in the heart of a child, but the rod of discipline drives it far from him."

Proverbs 23:13 "Do not withhold discipline from a child; if you strike him with a rod, he will not die."

Proverbs 23:22 "Listen to your father who gave you life, and do not despise your mother when she is old."

Proverbs 23:24–25 "The father of the righteous will greatly rejoice; he who fathers a wise son will be glad in him. Let your father and mother be glad; let her who bore you rejoice."

Proverbs 29:15 "The rod and reproof give wisdom, but a child left to himself brings shame to his mother."

Proverbs 29:17 "Discipline your son, and he will give you rest; he will give delight to your heart".

Ephesians 6:1–4 "Children, obey your parents in the Lord, for this is right. 'Honor your father and mother' (this is the first commandment with a promise), 'that it may go well with you and that you may live long in the land.' Fathers, do not provoke your children to anger, but bring them up in the discipline and instruction of the LORD."

Colossians 3:20–21 "Children, obey your parents in everything, for this pleases the LORD. Fathers, do not provoke your children, lest they become discouraged."

1 Thessalonians 2:11–12 "For you know how, like a father with his children, we exhorted each one of you and encouraged you and charged you to walk in a manner worthy of God, who calls you into his own kingdom and glory."

1 Timothy 5:8 "But if anyone does not provide for his relatives, and especially for members of his household, he has denied the faith and is worse than an unbeliever."

Hebrews 12:7 "It is for discipline that you have to endure. God is treating you as sons. For what son is there whom his father does not discipline?"

*All verses are English Standard Version unless noted

**THE WORD
AND
FATHERHOOD**

CHECK OUT OTHER VOLUMES OF

THE SERIES™

Volume 1
A Man and His Design

Volume 2
A Man and His Story

Volume 3
A Man and His Traps

Volume 4
A Man and His Work

Volume 5
A Man and His Marriage

Volume 6
A Man and His Fatherhood

Purchase Individual Sessions and Entire Volumes at

authenticmanhood.com

SESSION SIX | DECISIONS

SCRIPTURE REFERENCES

Proverbs 13:20 (ESV) "Whoever walks with the wise becomes wise, but the companion of fools will suffer harm."

Romans 8:28 (ESV) "And we know that for those who love God all things work together for good, for those who are called according to his purpose."

Ephesians 6:4 (ESV) "Fathers, do not provoke your children to anger, but bring them up in the discipline and instruction of the Lord."

Proverbs 9:10 (ESV) "The fear of the LORD is the beginning of wisdom, and the knowledge of the Holy One is insight."

Colossians 1:16-17 (ESV) "For by him all things were created, in heaven and on earth, visible and invisible, whether thrones or dominions or rulers or authorities—all things were created through him and for him. And he is before all things, and in him all things hold together."

Psalm 119:105 (ESV) "Your word is a lamp to my feet and a light to my path."

Hebrews 13:20-21 (ESV) "Now may the God of peace who brought again from the dead our Lord Jesus, the great shepherd of the sheep, by the blood of the eternal covenant, equip you with everything good that you may do his will, working in us that which is pleasing in his sight, through Jesus Christ, to whom be glory forever and ever. Amen."

ACTION PLAN

YOUR STRATEGIC MOVE | SESSION ONE : FOUNDATIONS

_____

_____

YOUR STRATEGIC MOVE | SESSION TWO : GRACE BASED

_____

_____

YOUR STRATEGIC MOVE | SESSION THREE : TRUE GREATNESS

_____

_____

YOUR STRATEGIC MOVE | SESSION FOUR : SONS

_____

_____

YOUR STRATEGIC MOVE | SESSION FIVE : DAUGHTERS

_____

_____

YOUR STRATEGIC MOVE | SESSION SIX : DECISIONS

_____

_____

A Man and His Fatherhood – Answer Key

SESSION ONE: FOUNDATION

I. 2. easy
    3. cultivating
II. 1. God's
    • gift
    • life
    2. commission
    3. intentionality
    4. heart
       • toxic
          ° external
          ° heart
    5.
       • brokenness
       •forgiveness
       •grace

SESSION TWO: GRACE BASED

I.   1. heart
II. 1.
        • fear
     3. Grace
        • grace
        • God
III. 1. Different
        • grace
     2. vulnerable
        •mask
     3. candid
        • deflate
        • respectfully
     4. mistakes
        • grace

SESSION THREE: TRUE GREATNESS

I.   1. course

4. success
5. self-absorbed
II. others

III.
     1. humble
     2. grateful
     3. generous
     4. servant's
IV.
     1. examples
     3. opportunities
V.
     1. mission
        • God's
     2. mate
     3. master

SESSION FOUR: SONS

I.   nurtures
     growing
     framework

II. 1. Understanding
        • temperament
     2. Engaging
        l. engaged
           • side
           • wrestle
           • enjoyment
           • heart
           • strength
           • pursuits
           • quality

          • *consultant*

   3. *Validation*

   4. *Initiating, Celebrating*

          • *fundamental*

          • *celebrated*

III.

   1.

          • *present*

          power

SESSION FIVE: DAUGHTERS

I.   1. *important*

      2. *different*

      4. *solid*

          • *template*

      5.

          • *impact*

      6.

          • *listen*

          • *words*

          • *change*

          • *shaped*

      7. *faith*

      8. *fight*

      9. *affection*

          • *personally*

• *good*

• *ongoing*

5.

• *unrushed*

• *fun*

• *rhythms*

6.

   • *over-discipline*

7.

• *ultimate*

• *grace*

SESSION SIX: DECISIONS

I.   *unity*

II.   1.

          •*reality*

          • *offense*

     2.

          • *benefical*

          • *Equip*

     3.

          • *choice*

          • *responsible*

     4.